# The Red Merit Badge of Courage
**A Short Play for Young Actors**

by Nicolas Hoover

Single copies of plays are sold for reading purposes only. The copying or duplicating of a play, or any part of play, by hand or by any other process, is an infringement of the copyright. Such infringement will be vigorously prosecuted.

**Baker's Plays**
**7611 Sunset Blvd.**
**Los Angeles, CA 90042**
bakersplays.com

## NOTICE

This book is offered for sale at the price quoted only on the understanding that, if any additional copies of the whole or any part are necessary for its production, such additional copies will be purchased. The attention of all purchasers is directed to the following: this work is fully protected under the copyright laws of the United States of America, the British Commonwealth, including Canada, and all other countries of the Copyright Union. Violations of the Copyright Law are punishable by fine or imprisonment, or both. The copying or duplication of this work or any part of this work, by hand or by any process, is an infringement of the copyright and will be vigorously prosecuted.

This play may not be produced by amateurs or professionals for public or private performance without first submitting application for performing rights. Licensing fees are due on all performances whether for charity or gain, or whether admission is charged or not. Since performance of this play without the payment of the licensing fee renders anybody participating liable to severe penalties imposed by the law, anybody acting in this play should be sure, before doing so, that the licensing fee has been paid. Professional rights, reading rights, radio broadcasting, television and all mechanical rights, etc. are strictly reserved. Application for performing rights should be made directly to BAKER'S PLAYS.

No one shall commit or authorize any act or omission by which the copyright of, or the right to copyright, this play may be impaired. No one shall make any changes in this play for the purpose of production.

Publication of this play does not imply availability for performance. Both amateurs and professionals considering a production are strongly advised in their own interest to apply to Baker's Plays for written permission before starting rehearsals, advertising, or booking a theatre.

Whenever the play is produced, the author's name must be carried in all publicity, advertising and programs. Also, the following notice must appear on all printed programs, "Produced by special arrangement with Baker's Plays."

Licensing fees for THE RED MERIT BADGE OF COURAGE are based on a per performance rate and payable one week in advance of the production.

Please consult the Baker's Plays website at www.bakersplays.com or our current print catalogue for up to date licensing fee information.

Copyright © 2010 by Nicolas Hoover
Made in U.S.A.
All rights reserved.

THE RED MERIT BADGE OF COURAGE
ISBN **978-0-87440-392-3**
#2072-B

# CHARACTERS

FIRESIDE SCOUTS TROOP #182:
**ELLE "THE VETERAN" SANDERS** - the most experienced
**MELISSA "THE BOOKWORM" TURNER** - an avid reader
**ELIZABETH "THE DICTIONARY" MATTHEWS** - a walking dictionary
**KJ "THE LIP" GARCIA** - a sarcastic wit
**ROSE "THE COMPASS" PETERS** - can get anywhere with a map
**LUCY "THE STOMACH" ANDERSON** - always hungry

THE MARSHMALLOWS (the youngest Fireside Scouts):
**ANDREA**
**NORA**
**BRIANNA**

TWO TREES:
**RED** - a cedar
**NEEDLES** - a pine

THE ADULTS:
**NARRATOR** - very bad at his job
**STAGE MANAGER** - very good at her job
**MRS. HENDERSON** - very old and practically blind (played by the Stage Manager)

# PLACE
Yellowstone National Park.

# TIME
Summer.

## AUTHOR'S NOTE

Actors remain on stage between scenes unless indicated by a stage direction. Scene breaks indicate a new story element rather than a break in the action, which is continuous. Scene titles may be projected above the stage or placed on placards or read aloud by the **NARRATOR**.

### Scene One: The Predicament

*(AT RISE: The **GIRLS** of Fireside Scouts Troop #182 huddle together in some suggestion of a forest, while the **NARRATOR** sits comfortably in an overstuffed armchair off to the side of the stage.)*

*(**THE FIRESIDE SCOUTS** scream in unison: a piercing, earsplitting scream that goes on for an uncomfortably long time.)*

**NARRATOR.** The girls of Fireside Scouts Troop # 182 were lost.

*(**THE FIRESIDE SCOUTS** scream again for good measure.)*

**ELLE.** Hold it! The girls of Fireside Scouts Troop # 182 are never lost.

**KJ.** We're lost. The narrator said so.

**ELLE.** The narrator doesn't know what he's talking about. What is our motto?

**KJ.** "As soon as something unexpected happens freak out?"

**ELLE.** No. Elizabeth, what is our motto?

**ELIZABETH.** "Prepare yourself."

**ELLE.** Exactly. And how long have we been preparing ourselves? Huh!?

**MELISSA.** A year.

**LUCY.** A month.

**NORA.** A day and a half.

**ELLE.** Exactly! It doesn't matter how long you've been a fireside scout. It matters how long *I've* been a fireside scout. And I've been a fireside scout for six years. And I've been waiting six years for an opportunity like this: an opportunity to put my vast knowledge of earning merit badges to the test! I've earned hundreds of merit badges and we're going to find our way back to the camp before it gets dark.

**BRIANNA.** How?

**ELLE.** With the map that Rose is holding in her hands.

**ROSE.** I don't have a map.

**ELLE.** What happened to it?

**ROSE.** Lucy ate it.

**FIRESIDE SCOUTS.** Lucy!

**LUCY.** I was hungry.

**ELLE.** That's no excuse. What is number 41 in the Fireside Scout Code?

**KJ.** "Never eat the map?"

**ELLE.** No. Elizabeth, what is number 41 in the Fireside Scout Code?

**ELIZABETH.** "Wear socks."

**ELLE.** I'm sorry, number 42.

**ELIZABETH.** "The map will guide the way."

**ELLE.** How can it guide you if you eat it?

**ROSE.** It can't.

**ELLE.** It can't.

**ROSE.** What are we going to do?!!

**MELISSA.** Hold it! What about the exposition?

**LUCY.** Exposition?

**MELISSA.** Every good story begins with exposition.

**ANDREA.** What is exposition?

**ELIZABETH.** Exposition: the part of a story that provides the background information needed to understand the characters and the action.

**MELISSA.** The narrator isn't doing his job.

*(They all glare at the **NARRATOR**.)*

**NARRATOR.** Sorry.

## Scene Two: Exposition

**NARRATOR.** Introducing: Fireside Scouts Troop # 182!

*(As each girl introduces herself, she steps forward and poses, as if in a fashion show.)*

**ELLE.** Elle "The Veteran" Sanders.

**NARRATOR.** Elle has been a Fireside Scout longer than anyone in the troop and she has the entire Fireside Scout Code completely memorized.

**MELISSA.** Melissa "The Bookworm" Turner.

**NARRATOR.** Melissa also has the Fireside Scout Code completely memorized, but that's because she's completely memorized every book she's ever read.

**ELIZABETH.** Elizabeth "The Dictionary" Matthews.

**NARRATOR.** Elizabeth can define anything.

**ELIZABETH.** Anything: any object, occurrence, or matter whatsoever. Anything.

**KJ.** KJ "The Lip" Garcia.

**NARRATOR.** KJ can't resist wit and sarcasm, applying them liberally but evenly to a variety of situations.

**KJ.** *(sarcastically)* I'm not sarcastic at all. I don't know what you're talking about.

**ROSE.** Rose "The Compass" Peters.

**NARRATOR.** Rose can find her way anywhere with a map. If there is a map.

**LUCY.** Lucy "The Stomach" Anderson.

**NARRATOR.** Lucy is always hungry.

**LUCY.** I'm hungry.

**EVERYONE ELSE.** We know.

**NARRATOR.** And the youngest Fireside Scouts, lovingly called marshmallows.

**ANDREA.** Andrea.

**NORA.** Nora.

**BRIANNA.** Brianna.

**ANDREA.** Why are we called marshmallows?

*(beat)*

**NARRATOR.** Because you're small, squishy, and uh…burst into flame easily when held over a campfire?

*(The **MARSHMALLOWS** scream.)*

**ELLE.** Not only are you an awful narrator, you have a sick sense of humor. We do not hold marshmallows over a fire, well…I mean we hold real marshmallows over the fire –

*(The **MARSHMALLOWS** scream.)*

– but never children.

**NARRATOR.** So why are they called marshmallows?

**ROSE.** Because their uniforms are white instead of beige.

**ELIZABETH.** Taupe.

**ROSE.** What's the difference?

**ELIZABETH.** Beige is grayish-brown whereas taupe is brownish-gray.

**NARRATOR.** Alright, so they know the characters. Now what?

**MELISSA.** Tell them how we got lost in the woods. Duh.

### Scene Three: How Troop #182 Got Lost in the Woods

**NARRATOR.** It was a beautiful day as the girls of Fireside Scouts Troop #182 drove deep into Yellowstone National Park in their van.

**ELLE.** What a beautiful day.

**BRIANNA.** The birds.

**NORA.** The flowers.

**ANDREA.** The poison ivy.

**LUCY.** I'm hungry.

**NARRATOR.** Everyone else was hungry, too.

**EVERYONE ELSE.** We're hungry, too.

**NARRATOR.** So, they stopped for lunch. But Mrs. Henderson, their scout leader, being deaf and mostly blind, drove off with a van that she thought was full of screaming girls but was in fact empty.

## Scene Four: Searching for Food

**MELISSA.** What are we going to do?

**ELLE.** Follow the code. Who can tell me what rule number one of the Fireside Scout Code is?

**KJ.** "Sell cookies?"

**ELLE.** "We may be worthless as individuals, but together we can do anything."

**ROSE.** Yeah, we have to work together.

**ELLE.** Look: we may be stuck in the middle of Yellowstone National Park without our scout leader or a map, but we're Fireside Scouts and we can do anything if we work together.

**LUCY.** I'm hungry.

**ELLE.** You're always hungry.

**MARSHMALLOWS.** We're hungry, too.

**ELLE.** But we just ate. What is rule number 35 of the Fireside Scout Code?

**KJ.** Never argue with Elle or she'll quote the Fireside Scout Code?

**ELLE.** For your information: rule number 35 is "eat only when necessary" and why are you even here? All you ever do is make sarcastic comments.

**KJ.** My parents forced me to do it. They thought it would be enriching. I fail to see how any of this is "enriching."

**ELIZABETH.** Well, enriching has multiple definitions.

**KJ.** Uh oh.

**ELIZABETH.** It can mean to make rich or richer.

**ROSE.** That's why we sell cookies!

**ELIZABETH.** It also means, of course, "to make fuller, more meaningful, or more rewarding," which is what your parents probably meant.

**KJ.** And none of this is making anything fuller, more meaningful, or more rewarding.

**ELIZABETH.** It also means to fertilize (like soil) or add nutrients (like milk).

**ROSE.** And they do feed us.

**LUCY.** I'm hungry.

**ROSE.** Have a marshmallow.

*(The **MARSHMALLOWS** scream.)*

**ELIZABETH.** It also means to add to the beauty of something.

**ROSE.** That's why we braid each other's hair.

**ELIZABETH.** And last but not least: enriching means to increase the amount of radioactive isotopes in a material.

**KJ.** That sounds a little more interesting.

**ELIZABETH.** I think this whole thing is very enriching in multiple ways.

**MELISSA.** Excuse me, but none of this is moving the plot forward. Hey, Narrator, you have to keep us on course.

**NARRATOR.** Right. They quickly found food, and –

**MELISSA.** No, no, no: we need a sense of impending doom, you have to foreshadow.

**NARRATOR.** What in the world is foreshadow?

**ELIZABETH.** Foreshadow...

**KJ.** You just had to ask, didn't you?

**ELIZABETH.** ...To present an indication or suggestion beforehand.

**KJ.** Is that English?

**MELISSA.** In other words: you have to let the audience know that something bad is about to happen.

**NARRATOR.** Like this? While Troop #182 searched for food, KJ was planning a way to get back at her parents, and at the same time, scare the merit badges off all the other Fireside Scouts.

**KJ.** *(to audience)* My parents are going to be sorry they made me do this. When it gets dark I'm going to scare these wimps more than they've ever been scared before.

**MELISSA.** *Now* move the plot along.

**NARRATOR.** They worked together to find food.

**ELLE.** What food do we have with us?

**KJ.** We have marshmallows.

(*The* **MARSHMALLOWS** *scream.*)

**ROSE.** But Lucy already ate all of them.

**KJ.** I don't mean *those* marshmallows. I mean *them*.

(*beat*)

(*The* **MARSHMALLOWS** *scream.*)

**ROSE.** Elle, what are we going to do?

**ELLE.** I don't know. Hey, Narrator! What are we going to do?

**NARRATOR.** Most of the troop survived on berries, but Lucy managed to catch squirrels and chipmunks to satisfy her insatiable hunger.

**ELLE.** Now that everyone is wellfed, I think the Fireside Scout Code might be able to tell us what to do in a situation like this. Can anyone think of what that is?

**KJ.** No.

**ELLE.** Number 56: "When you get lost stay in one place." Let's set up camp!

## Scene Five: That's When It Started to Rain

**NARRATOR.** That's when it started to rain.

(**THE FIRESIDE SCOUTS** *scream.*)

**ELLE.** Quick! Run for those trees over there!

**NARRATOR.** They took shelter under a pair of trees.

(**RED** *and* **NEEDLES** *enter, their backs to the audience, and the* **SCOUTS** *huddle under their branches.*)

**ELLE.** Does anyone have a tent?

**BRIANNA.** I do.

**ELLE.** You do?

**BRIANNA.** But it's very small.

**ELLE.** Does anyone else have a tent?

*(silence)*

Give me your tent.

**NARRATOR.** Some of the Fireside Scouts worked together to set up the tent, while the rest gathered firewood. Hey, Melissa!

**MELISSA.** What?

**NARRATOR.** What do I do if I have to go to the bathroom?

**MELISSA.** Can't you hold it?

**NARRATOR.** No. Can you cover for me?

**MELISSA.** I'm a character in your story. I can't narrate my own story.

**NARRATOR.** Why not?

**ELLE.** What's the trouble over here?

**NARRATOR.** No trouble.

**ELLE.** Then why aren't you gathering firewood, Melissa?

**MELISSA.** This so-called Narrator over here didn't go to the bathroom before we left.

**NARRATOR.** I didn't have to go then.

**ELLE.** Melissa, what is rule number 126 of the Fireside Scout Code?

**MELISSA.** "Go to the bathroom before you leave."

**ELLE.** "Go to the bathroom before you leave."

**NARRATOR.** Look, I'm sorry, I'll make it up to you: I'll give you a happy ending!

**MELISSA.** You were already going to give us a happy ending. We're children. This is a children's story. Happy endings are a requirement. You could at least know your own genre!

**NARRATOR.** I'll just be a second.

**LUCY.** Can you bring back some food?

**NARRATOR.** Is that allowed?

**MELISSA.** No.

**NARRATOR.** What do I do? I can't hold it any longer.

**MELISSA.** Find someone to take your place. Someone who *isn't* in the story.

**NARRATOR.** Good idea.

*(NARRATOR exits and returns with the STAGE MANAGER.)*

**STAGE MANAGER.** What are you doing? I'm not supposed to be out here. I'm the Stage Manager.

**NARRATOR.** I just have to go to the bathroom.

**STAGE MANAGER.** What am I supposed to do?

**NARRATOR.** Stall. The girls are setting up the tent and gathering firewood.

**FIRESIDE SCOUTS.** We are?

**NARRATOR.** Yes. Go!

*(They go. To STAGE MANAGER:)*

Make it interesting.

*(NARRATOR exits.)*

**STAGE MANAGER.** *(calling after him)* Wait! I have no idea what I'm doing!

**NARRATOR.** *(offstage)* Neither do I!

### Scene Six: Stalling

*(STAGE MANAGER stares at the audience, trying to think of something.)*

**STAGE MANAGER.** Listen to the birds.
How lovely in the summer.
Their song is the wind.

**MELISSA.** I hardly think this is the time for haikus!

**STAGE MANAGER.** Aren't you supposed to be collecting firewood?

**MELISSA.** Maybe.

**STAGE MANAGER.** Then get to work.

*(to the audience)*

I hate Girlscouts.

**MELISSA.** We're not Girlscouts! We're Fireside Scouts!

**STAGE MANAGER.** Firewood. Now.

*(to the audience)*

Listen to the trees.
If only we could hear them.
What would they say?

*(into headset)*

Lighting Cue 27: Go.

*(Lights focus on NEEDLES and RED as they turn downstage to face the audience. FIRESIDE SCOUTS may exit for the following dialogue, remain in darkness, continue in slow motion, or freeze.)*

**NEEDLES.** I can't feel my arms.

**RED.** You don't have any arms.

**NEEDLES.** Right.

**RED.** You're a tree.

**NEEDLES.** Sometimes I forget.

**RED.** You're a cone head, you know that?

**NEEDLES.** I may be a tree, but I still have feelings.

**RED.** You have feeling. Singular.

**NEEDLES.** I have a wide range of emotions.

**RED.** They just all look the same to an outside observer.

**NEEDLES.** I can't believe they've gotten to you.

**RED.** Here it comes.

**NEEDLES.** They want you to believe that you're only a tree. You're more than that, you're alive.

**RED.** Don't you get started with all that transcendental sap.

**NEEDLES.** You have feelings, you have depth, you deserve life. They want to reduce you to 2 by 4, to a commodity. You've got to stand up and believe, like me, that you are a rich, complex, dimensional being, worthy of life. Will you let them profit from your demise?

**RED.** I'm just willing to sacrifice myself for the greater good.

**NEEDLES.** Wood.

**RED.** What?

**NEEDLES.** Make no mistake: wood is all you're dying for.

**RED.** I wish you would go away.

**NEEDLES.** I can't just leave you here alone.

**RED.** That's because you don't have any legs.

**NEEDLES.** Unless I leave on a truck.

**RED.** You can drive?

**NEEDLES.** A lumber truck.

**RED.** Way to dampen the mood. I start to smell when I get damp.

**NEEDLES.** Funny.

**RED.** I just made my first pun.

**NEEDLES.** Sap.

**RED.** I think I'm blushing.

**NEEDLES.** So, you're going to just sit there?

**RED.** Do I have a choice?

**NEEDLES.** They're cutting down our neighbors like grass! And you're making jokes?!!

**RED.** You're right. We have to do something.

**NEEDLES.** Alright. What are we going to do?

**RED.** I'm stumped. That's my second pun.

**NEEDLES.** Congratulations.

**RED.** I'm just popping them out now, one after another.

**NEEDLES.** They're coming for you.

**RED.** They are not.

**NEEDLES.** I hear them.

**RED.** You're being paranoid.

**NEEDLES.** I see them.

**RED.** I don't see anything.

**NEEDLES.** I'm taller than you are.

**RED.** You're a pine in my trunk. That's three.

**NEEDLES.** Your jokes are getting worse.

**RED.** I'm new at this.

**NEEDLES.** The hill is bald. Vacant. All around us, except for us. They're coming for us next. One day you'll be asleep. You'll awaken to a sound that drowns out everything. And then silence. You'll be alone. And it will be too late.

**RED.** You're overreacting.

**NEEDLES.** Ahhhhhhhhhhhhhhhhhhhhhhhhhhhhhhhhhhhhhhhhhhhhhh!

**RED.** Funny. Hey, Listen. Do you want to go bowling on Wednesday? Oh, that's right, never mind: I'm a Cedar. Cedars are notoriously bad bowlers. My grandfather tried bowling once and the best he could get was a split. Hah! Get it? A split?

*(beat)*

Needles? Are you still there? Stop fooling around or I'm leafing.

*(beat)*

Oh come on, that was funny. Leafing?

*(beat)*

**RED.** *(cont.)* Needles? This isn't funny anymore.

*(beat)*

You're giving me the silent treatment, aren't you? I probably deserve it. I'm sorry.

*(beat)*

Stop this, you're really freaking me out.

**NEEDLES.** Boo!

**RED.** That wasn't funny. You scared the sap out of me!

**NEEDLES.** Sorry.

*(beat)*

Hey, uh, Red? Do you smell something burning?

**STAGE MANAGER.** *(into headset)* Lighting Cue 28: Go.

*(**RED** and **NEEDLES** turn upstage as lights return to normal.)*

*(to audience)*

The girls had finished setting up the tent, which they did all fit in, though snugly.

*(The **FIRESIDE SCOUTS**, except **KJ**, huddle in the tent, which barely fits them all.)*

The girls had also started a campfire. It was a good thing, too, because it was dark. Very dark.

*(into headset)*

Lighting Cue 29: Go.

**ELLE.** Nice work, troop. We have managed to survive in the wilderness for exactly five hours and twenty seven minutes. And we achieved this by working together. Now that we have a campfire, I'm sure we can make it through the night without being eaten by a bear.

**STAGE MANAGER.** That's when they realized KJ was gone.

**LUCY.** Hey, where's KJ?

*(**KJ** screams offstage. An ominous, blood-curdling scream that goes on for an uncomfortably long time.)*

*(beat)*

*(The other* **FIRESIDE SCOUTS** *scream.)*

*(beat)*

*(***RED*** and* **NEEDLES** *turn downstage and scream.)*

*(***NARRATOR*** enters.)*

**NARRATOR.** *(to* **STAGE MANAGER***)* Alright. You can go back to whatever it is you do.

**STAGE MANAGER.** No.

**NARRATOR.** What do you mean "no"?

**STAGE MANAGER.** I'm just starting to enjoy this.

**NARRATOR.** So? It's *my* job.

**STAGE MANAGER.** That you dumped on *me*.

**NARRATOR.** Temporarily.

**STAGE MANAGER.** Temporarily or not, you gave it to me, and I'm not giving it back.

**NARRATOR.** I had to go to the bathroom.

**STAGE MANAGER.** Why didn't you go before we started the show?

**NARRATOR.** I didn't have to go then.

**MELISSA.** You people! Just when we start to build up some momentum, some suspense, you two totally *waste* it.

**NARRATOR.** Yeah. Stop wasting the momentum. Whatever that is.

**STAGE MANAGER.** Fine. I quit.

*(She hands him her headset.)*

**NARRATOR.** Wait! You still have to…do…whatever it is you do!

**STAGE MANAGER.** Figure it out!

**NARRATOR.** You're under contract!

*(The* **STAGE MANAGER** *exits.)*

Where were we?

**MELISSA.** We were at the climax, and then you ruined it.

**NARRATOR.** Sorry. The Fireside Scouts gathered firewood.

**MELISSA.** We're way past that.

**NARRATOR.** They built a fire.

**MELISSA.** Past that.

**ELLE.** I congratulated everyone on surviving for more then five hours.

**LUCY.** And then I noticed that KJ was missing.

**MELISSA.** And then–

>   (**KJ** *screams offstage.*)
>
>   (*beat*)
>
>   (*The* **OTHER FIRESIDE SCOUTS** *scream.*)
>
>   (*beat*)
>
>   (**RED** *and* **NEEDLES** *turn downstage and scream.*)

**NARRATOR.** Wow, that is suspenseful.

>   (**KJ** *jumps out.*)

**KJ.** BOO!

>   (*Everyone, including the* **NARRATOR**, *screams.*)

Hah! I got you! I knew I could scare the merit badges off you. You're all a bunch of sissies.

>   (*a sound*)

**ELLE.** What was that?

**NARRATOR.** Don't look at me, I didn't do it.

**MELISSA.** That sounded like an ursus arctos.

**LUCY.** A what?

**MELISSA.** An ursus arctos: a grizzly bear.

>   (**KJ** *dives in the tent with the others, as a shadow appears on the back of the tent: it grows and grows, as the* **FIRESIDE SCOUTS** *become more and more frightened and huddle more and more closely together in the very small tent.*)

## Scene Seven: The Bear

*(The tent opens.)*

*(The* **FIRESIDE SCOUTS** *scream.)*

*(But it is only* **MRS. HENDERSON**.*)*

**MRS. HENDERSON.** Hello, dears. Did you all have a lovely evening?

**NARRATOR.** Mrs. Henderson had finally found them. The end.

**MELISSA.** Hold on!

**NARRATOR.** What?

**MELISSA.** That's it? That's the end?

**NARRATOR.** Does it matter?

**MELISSA.** It needs a climax, or a celebration, or at least a moral.

**NARRATOR.** Alright.

## Scene Eight: And the Moral of the Story Is

**MRS. HENDERSON.** And what did you all learn?

**ROSE.** I learned to always prepare myself for the worst.

**ELLE.** As number 76 of the Fireside Scout Code says: "Leadership is more than making decisions. You have to actually know things."

**BRIANNA.** I just had fun.

**NORA.** Me, too!

**ANDREA.** It would have been better if Mrs. Henderson was really a bear.

**LUCY.** I'm hungry.

**KJ.** I learned that while revenge is fun, it's more fun to have friends.

**MELISSA.** I learned to bring a good book.

**ELIZABETH.** This whole adventure could have been a little more succinct.

**KJ.** Why don't you use words that people understand?

**ELIZABETH.** Succinct: characterized by clear, precise expression in few words.

**MELISSA.** Speaking of succinct…narrator?

**NARRATOR.** And they all earned a thousand merit badges.

*(Nothing happens. The lights stay on. Everyone looks at the NARRATOR.)*

What?

*(The NARRATOR notices the headset.)*

Oh. How do I work this thing?

*(MRS. HENDERSON, reveals herself as the STAGE MANAGER, crosses to the NARRATOR, and takes the headset.)*

I thought you quit.

**STAGE MANAGER.** Do you want me to?

**NARRATOR.** No.

**STAGE MANAGER.** Then maybe you should start appreciating me.

**NARRATOR.** I do.

**STAGE MANAGER.** So, why don't you say "Thank you."

**NARRATOR.** Thank you?

**STAGE MANAGER.** And mean it.

**NARRATOR.** I couldn't do this without you.

**STAGE MANAGER.** That's right.

**NARRATOR.** And I really appreciate everything that you do.

  *(beat)*

**STAGE MANAGER.** *(into headset)* Lighting Cue 30: Go.

  *(Lights fade to black.)*

## End of Play

www.ingramcontent.com/pod-product-compliance
Lightning Source LLC
Chambersburg PA
CBHW072340300426
44109CB00043B/1968